MINNESOTA

MINNESOTA

PHOTOGRAPHY BY RON VAN ZEE

TEXT BY IVAN KUBISTA

International Standard Book Number 0-912856-23-8
Library of Congress Catalog Number 75-41888
Copyright© 1976 by Graphic Arts Center Publishing Co.
2000 N.W. Wilson • Portland, Oregon 97209 • 503/224-7777
Publisher • Charles H. Belding
Designer • Robert Reynolds
Text • Ivan Kubista
Printer • Graphic Arts Center
Binding • Lincoln & Allen
Printed in the United States of America
Third Printing

1812-1866

Dedicated with respect to the memory of Father Lucien Galtier, who left his native France to become a missionary in the Minnesota wilds. In 1841 he built a crude log church near Fort Snelling and enshrined it to Saint Paul, from which the city took its name. His tenacity and courage left an indelible mark on this bountiful and wonderful state.

Morning sun generates a brilliant glow on
box elder foliage. This area may have been the scene
of a battle between the Chippewa and Sioux.

Hiking along edge of the Minnesota River
Valley near New Prague. It is one of the many scenic
and picturesque valleys within the state.

Hillside spring meandering down gentle slope to
eventually enter the Mississippi River. Pages 8 and 9:
White caps reveal severity of wind along
south shore of Lake of the Woods near Warroad.

Clear water of Lake Itasca spills over rocky
ledge giving birth to the mighty Mississippi River.
It will travel 2,459 miles creating boundaries
or parts of boundaries to ten states prior to entering
the Gulf of Mexico.

Ducks and gulls feeding in the quiet water
near lighthouse at Grand Marais on Lake Superior.

Winter landscape along the Cascade
River, on north shore of Lake Superior near Tofte.

Brilliant glow of the rising sun marks
the beginning of another day in the harbor
area of Duluth.

Early evening reflections on surface
of the placid St. Louis River near Eveleth.

Barn reflects concern for permanence
and feasibility on farm near Zumbro Falls.

The transfer site is now a state wayside park, seldom visited except by locals, called Old Crossing Treaty.

Among the people of northwest Minnesota, however, is a general belief that white civilization penetrated the region before—as long ago as the mid-fourteenth century.

The focus of this belief is a large rock, now displayed in the Runestone Museum of Alexandria, on which is inscribed a dated account of Viking explorers in trouble. The runic letters have been translated to read:

"(We are) eight Goths and 22 Norwegians on (an) exploration journey from Vinland through the west. We had camp (by a lake with) two skerries one day's journey north from this stone. We were (out) and fished one day. After we came home (we) found ten men red with blood and dead. Ave Maria save (us) from evil."

On the edge of the stone are the following words:

"(We) have ten men by the sea to look after our ships 14 days' journeys from this island. (In the) year (of our Lord) 1362."

The now-famous runestone was unearthed near Kensington in 1898 by Olof Ohman, a farmer who found it entangled in the roots of a tree he was clearing. Since then, historians have had to grapple with the problem of its authenticity and its implications that Viking explorations in Minnesota preceded Columbus by 130 years!

Some favorably disposed scholars like to recount other historical "evidence." Such as a Viking sword exhumed near the little town of Ulen; an ancient Norse ceremonial halberd found among tree roots near Climax; a firesteel buried on the shores of Cormorant Lake; a score of mooring stones discovered on lake shores and rivers, and other—perhaps more dubious—runestones.

There are, of course, deflating questions asked by Viking theory detractors. Is the Ulen sword really nothing more than a rusty 1861 Navy cutlass? Is the Norse halberd a 19th century store display relic designed to promote Battle Ax chewing tobacco? Are the mooring stones mere debris left by early road builders who bored them to hold dynamite charges? Is the runestone itself an elaborate hoax?

Perhaps. Perhaps not. But while scholars are split fairly evenly on the subject, one haunting fact remains.

The Mandan Indians, a small North Dakota tribe (extinct since a smallpox plague near the turn of the century), startled their white discoverers with their blue eyes, their dwellings—more akin to 14th century Scandinavian huts than to any hogans or teepees—and their acquaintance with such Christian concepts as the virgin birth and a crucified saviour.

Wherever the truth lies, the Viking stories lend historic color to a region already wealthy in pioneer and Indian lore; and the sight of an ancient, inscribed rock in a museum has an attraction for thousands of tourists who contribute heavily to the local economy each year.

That appeal, however, is by no means the only reason for the swollen summer traffic. More important are the thousands of lakes which have spawned not only great numbers of game fish, but a myriad of summer resorts hosting vacationers from every state.

Even so, hospitality is a relatively new industry. Most major cities outside the Red River Valley were born in the lumbering boom of the late 19th and early 20th centuries. But as the vast pine forests dwindled, so did the loggers with their ever-ready surpluses of cash. Unlike the fate common to the old west cattle towns, however, Minnesota's communities managed to parlay their natural resources into a winning economic hand—the tourist trade.

The successful transition is apparent in towns like Bemidji, Brainerd, Walker, Wadena or Detroit Lakes. While each has its share of manufacturing and agricultural-oriented industries to provide a stable economic base, it has been the green forests, the canoe rivers, the walleye lakes and the crisp, clean air which have generated the impetus for growth. Or, if not growth, at least survival!

There are also places, fortunately, where the terms "growth" and "development"—at least in the industrial sense—have little meaning. One of these is the Northwest Angle, the proper name for Minnesota's "chimney".

This cartographic oddity is, to the surprise of most people who see a detailed map of Minnesota, about 80% water. It encompasses most of Lake of the Woods, the state's largest, while its land mass is attached to Canada.

This patch of Minnesota is, in truth, a geographic mistake, included as part of the United States through ignorance at the time the Canadian boundaries were created.

The Treaty of 1783 stated that the boundary would extend through Lake of the Woods to its northernmost point—then due west to the Mississippi. When geographers realized the Mississippi did not come anywhere near Lake of the Woods, the treaty was changed to extend the boundary from the tip of the inlet in a straight line to the 49th parallel. The freakish result was about 130 square miles of American territory created in the northern wilderness, accessible only by boat, plane or—in winter—snowmobile.

Three small villages exist here: Angle Inlet, Oak Island and Penasse. The latter, until Alaska became a state, boasted the nation's northernmost post office.

A small amount of lumbering, some commercial fishing and an increasing tourist trade provide the sustenance for these Minnesotans. But it is enough. They place a high value on the natural beauty and superb recreation lands around them.

The lake itself is peppered with islands, whose rocky composition is no deterrent to the pine, spruce and lush forest foliage which manages to cover them. Some of them, in spite of their remoteness, even occupy important slots in Minnesota's history.

These waters were familiar to Frenchmen by the early 18th century and one, Pierre sieur de la Vérendrye, explored them intensely in an effort to find a route to the Pacific. In so doing, he built a chain of outposts from Minnesota's Rainy Lake into Saskatchewan. One of these, Fort St. Charles, has been restored to its 1732 appearance.

Located on Magnusson's Island, the fort is accessible via cruise boat from the Northwest Angle. Not far away, on another island, is where Father Jean-Pierre Alneau, a Jesuit priest, camped with a contingent of 19 voyageurs one night. All died in an attack by Indians and their remains later taken to the fort. The incident gave the island its present name—Massacre Island.

Today the waters are the scene of more cheerful incidents—boatloads of vacationing anglers proudly holding up stringers of walleyes or a Sunday sailor skillfully guiding his white-sailed craft between the islands and the unpredictable winds they cause. Both give way in winter to snowmobilers, who find the frozen lake an ideal spot to test their machines to the limit.

Going straight south from the Northwest Angle, Minnesota's development unfolds almost like a history lesson. First are the magnificent forests and unpolluted rivers around and above Red Lake, frequented by the Red Lake Indians whose traditions have resisted, as far as possible, the white man's penchant for change.

Below Red Lake are vast state forest lands and cities which still recall the lumbering heyday. Bemidji is one of these and is best known to children everywhere as the home of two famous statues—a giant Paul Bunyan and his faithful blue ox, Babe. Those heroic figures standing on the shores of Lake Bemidji have become as important in Minnesota folklore as Hiawatha and Joe Rolette.

Paul came to life as the central character in a series of promotional pamphlets issued by a lumbering company in Akeley. He was so effective that the company eventually published collections of Bunyan tales for distribution to the kiddies. After that, the character assumed an existence of his own, surviving forever the company whose products he was designed to advertise.

As the forests thin slightly, the number of lakes increases along with the population. Resort areas abound in friendly, touristy towns such as Walker, Pequot Lakes and Nisswa. Then comes Brainerd with its curious mixture of industry and tourist accommodations, followed by Little Falls, the home of Charles Lindbergh.

The Lindbergh home is preserved as part of the Charles A. Lindbergh State Park which, to the surprise of most, is not named for the famous aviator but for his father.

Charles, Senior, was a respected Minnesotan who served as a U.S. Congressman for ten years and authored three books on banking and finance. His home is open to visitors, but the lure is really in the mementoes it contains from his son's youth.

Upon reaching St. Cloud, the transition from the primitive to modern eras is complete. Known as the "granite city," its numerous stone quarries have provided building material for everything from churches and office buildings to schools and prison walls. A beehive of commerce, St. Cloud is the largest city before turning southeast toward the twin cities of St. Paul and Minneapolis.

Less than twenty miles west of St. Cloud is an unusual community called Collegeville. It is the site of St. John's University, Preparatory School, Seminary and Abbey—an entire community of students, monks and buildings dedicated to religion and education—administered by the Catholic Order of St. Benedict.

What stuns visitors to Collegeville is St. John's Church, a hypermodern structure designed by famed Hungarian architect Marcel Breuer big enough to seat 2,000—the entire population of the town.

A land of contrasts, this northwest quarter of Minnesota; in it is enough variety to satisfy any hankering for change. One can savor the green beauty of Lake Bronson State Park in Kittson County which has only five lakes . . . and explore the historic byways of Otter Tail County which has more than a thousand; see Indians harvest wild rice in a canoe, less than 100 miles from where giant combines race noisily through oceans of ripened wheat; tour the largest snowmobile manufacturing plant in the nation at Thief River Falls . . . only an hour away from where a photographer may be patiently waiting to photograph a moose in the wild; watch a Chippewa band stage a pow-wow on Lake Itasca, or enjoy the color of a Finnish festival in New York Mills; marvel at the estate of James J. Hill, the "empire builder" who fathered the Great Northern Railway, or follow a path around ancient Indian burial grounds; relax in the manicured beauty of Glenwood and its beautiful Lake Minnewaska, or visit the modest boyhood home of Sinclair Lewis in Sauk Centre—the town which served as a model for his most famous work, "Main Street."

Yet for all its color, the region as a whole is still just a piece of a larger Minnesota whose origins and character differ as much from those of the northwest as the various elements of the northwest vary among themselves. One of these areas begins just east of the central lakes region, and its personality began to change when cries of "gold" rang through the wilderness in 1865. Henry Eames, a geologist, touched off Minnesota's gold rush in the 1860's. He had taken soil samples near Lake Vermilion, about 25 miles west of present day Ely (pronounced ee'-lee), and a favorable assayer's report prompted him to go prospecting in a serious way.

Although Eames kept the report quiet, a St. Paul paper leaked word that he had discovered gold in the northern wilderness. The inevitable followed. Men took their savings, left their homes and succumbed to gold fever—only to meet with disappointment and despair with what developed as a futile quest.

Ignored during the furor were the traces of iron in the subsequent deluge of soil samples, and several years passed before George C. Stone, an imaginative Duluth resident, recognized the potential they represented. He eventually brought Minnesota's iron ore to the attention of Charlemagne Tower, a wealthy eastern industrialist.

Tower purchased land in the Lake Vermilion area, brought experienced men from the east, and soon began shipping ore from the Tower-Soudan mine—Minnesota's first. The rich ore there is now exhausted, but tourists can still view the ancient equipment in the haunted tunnels and find traces of the fool's gold that led Henry Eames and others astray.

Nearly a hundred years have elapsed since then, and the effects of iron—both good and bad—on Minnesota have been awesome.

Lying so very close to the surface, the state's iron ore is strip-mined (although Tower's mine was an underground operation for over 50 years). The result is a ravaged, pitted landscape that prompts headshaking and mutterings among those who love the natural, forested beauty peculiar to this part of the country.

Yet, the open-pit mines of the great iron ranges have a brutal kind of beauty all their own. The most spectacular is the Hull-Rust mine just outside of Hibbing.

Since the turn of the century, this colossal excavation—four miles long, two miles wide and 600 feet deep—has yielded over 600 million tons of ore, enough to fill 8.6 million railroad cars stretching more than one and a half times around the world.

The enormous iron resources of northeast Minnesota have been the greatest single contribution to the industrial growth of the nation (nearly two-thirds of its iron comes from Minnesota). At the same time, it continues to be an economic mainstay for descendants of the Finn and Norwegian settlers who made the industry possible.

Any description of the great iron ranges—there are three which combine to form a 140-mile zig-zag slash between Brainerd and Ely—suggests a region as desolate and crater-pocked as the surface of the moon. Such visions, however, are at odds with the reality.

And what is the reality? Again, Minnesota is a land of contrasts. Coexisting with mighty technologies that rip tons of ore from the earth and fabricate iron and steel for a nation are some of the most beautiful, unmolested natural areas found in that same nation.

The truth is that the visitor must often seek out the iron mines to view them. During routine travel, they are incidental breaks in the overwhelming ocean of great pine forests blanketing the entire northeastern quarter of the state.

If the voyageurs—those curious breeds of French adventurers whose cargo-laden canoes first penetrated this wilderness in the 18th century—were to return here, they would probably find little to make them ill-at-ease. After two centuries they could still walk through uninhabited forests, take fish from silent, crystal lakes, watch giant, black moose browsing in a swamp, and be lulled to sleep by distant, haunting cries of a loon.

As the Vikings and the Chippewa are an integral part of northwest

Minnesota lore, so is the voyageur legacy in the northeast. F. Lee Jaques, one of Minnesota's great painters, devoted much of his work to studies of voyageurs and the rugged lands in which they moved.

When the Congress approved development of a new national park in Minnesota, it was promptly called Voyageurs National Park.

And at the very tip of Minnesota's arrowhead is the Grand Portage National Monument, a restoration of the great fur depot whose log partitions once rang with the boisterous gatherings of voyageurs who came to collect wages from the North West Company.

The voyageurs are gone, of course, but the environment remains. Somehow, the very grandeur of the wilderness has given the most ardent, would-be "developers" reason to pause. The best illustration of this is the brief saga of Arthur Carhart.

In 1919 Carhart, a young landscape architect, was sent to the northern border lakes region by the U.S. Forest Service to lay the groundwork for a system of highways and associated recreation development in the far reaches of Superior National Forest.

The plan was to build roads to every lake in the forest and to encourage summer homes and campgrounds. So advanced was the project that money for it had already been appropriated.

But Carhart never turned in a road survey. Travelling the area by canoe, he was convinced that nothing man-made could ever enhance the place and would, in fact, degrade what already existed.

With a little eloquence and a great deal of courage, he explained to the Forest Service the importance of preserving such areas for future generations. Ultimately, the development plans were withdrawn in favor of a protection policy. The action saved what is now known as the Boundary Waters Canoe Area—a unique wilderness that attracts over 200,000 visitors each year.

What is so special about these lakes and forests to so impress a people accustomed to glass-steel-plastic environments? The answers go beyond the normal need for people to occasionally return to the land; they may even lie in the domains of psychology and religion.

Something in the human soul responds to the allure of these labyrinthine canoe passages—literally thousands of lakes whose expanse is broken by rugged, forested islands and great walls of primeval rock that defy the effects of millenia. There are still places where the teeming wildlife has not yet learned to regard humans as dangerous and the passing canoe merely attracts a puzzled glance from a shore-browsing deer or a gnawing beaver.

Some have described their visit as a return to the dawn of time, a moment when the artistry of the Creator so pleased Him that he ensured its existence, unchanged, forever.

The true wilderness of the northern boundary waters, however, is only a small part of Minnesota's scenic variety. If one searches only for forests and lakes, such ingredients make up the landscapes of other states in large quantity. Here, however, nature has provided some very special seasonings to set the state apart from all others.

Here, almost exclusively on the continent, the vast pine forests of the north spill over the Canadian border to meet the deciduous "Big Woods" that flourish upward from the south.

Not only do they meet, they mingle. And the effect is best appreciated in autumn when the eternal green of the softwoods becomes spattered with the gold, orange and red of hardwoods.

The easiest way to appreciate the phenomenon is to travel U.S. Hwy 61. between Grand Portage and Duluth during September. The route is laid out along the north shore of Lake Superior—often called America's "north coast."

On one side of the road are the lofty, craggy hills with their mantles of multicolored forests while, on the other, the icy waters of monstrous Lake Superior ceaselessly batter the impregnable granite cliffs which rise from the gravelled beaches.

About 40 miles below Grand Portage is the town of Grand Marais, still important as a rail departure point for logs harvested from the national forest (lumbering is second only to iron mining in industrial importance). Winding inland and northward from there is the Gunflint Trail, a well-paved county road that threads a tumultuous landscape of pines, lakes and rock formations toward secluded and picturesque fishing resorts.

But water is the pervading element here, and nature has used it unsparingly for creating extravagant displays. Chief among these, of course, is Lake Superior itself with its wild, tumbled shores. In the distance, one may see an ocean-going ship bound for the port of Duluth while, nearby, gulls wheel above the wakes of fishing boats. And beneath the waves, unseen, lie rusting and rotting hulks of many vessels whose captains underestimated the dangers of the north shore.

Until 1909 even the mute cliffs contributed to the hazards by deceiving ship compasses with their high content of iron ore. In that year, however, the Split Rock Lighthouse was completed and its great light and bellowing horn warned Great Lakes mariners of reefs and shallow waters for the next sixty years.

The lighthouse has outlived its usefuless with the advent of modern navigational aids, but it still operates intact as part of an unusual State Park. Some claim it is the most photographed lighthouse in the United States and its setting does much to support this contention.

Split Rock Lighthouse State Park is only one of nine parks dotting the north shore, each devoted to protecting a particularly striking scenic area. Most are on rivers whose names are as colorful as their scenery—Baptism, Cascade, Gooseberry, etc. One river is called the Temperance for its lack of sandbars or simply "bars." Nearly all have spectacular waterfalls and heavy populations of trout.

At the south end of the north shore drive is the bustling port city of Duluth, hosting vessels from all nations although it lies 1400 miles from the Atlantic. With a population of just over 100,000 it seems almost an enclave of cosmopolitan society in an area better known for forests, streams, Indian reservations and thousands of lakes.

The lakes increase in size and number westward from Duluth. There are so many, in fact, that of the 15,291 in the state almost a third have yet to be named. Others have names well-known to the nation's fishermen, however, and a trio of these—Cass, Leech and Lake Winnibigoshish—are famed as muskellunge lakes.

Serious muskie anglers are accustomed to the craftiness of this fish and often go for years without catching one. Thirty-inch muskies are too small to keep and 40-50 pound fish are not uncommon. The attraction, however, is to outwit the creatures which have been known to swim around with a lure in their mouths for an hour—then eject and depart while the hapless angler goes wild with frustration.

Another well-known lake is Mille Lacs Lake. It is a huge, oval, featureless body of relatively shallow water that has become a mecca for walleye fishermen. Walleye are not exactly difficult to catch, but their table qualities outweigh their lack of fight. Even in winter the lake is fished incessantly as whole cities of ice houses sprout across its frozen surface.

With all the fishing pressure, one marvels at how there can always be enough to go around. Yet, after decades of angling, the walleye populations continue to replenish themselves as abundantly as ever.

On the southeast shore of Mille Lacs Lake is Kathio, the oldest known village name in Minnesota. It is an Indian community originally inhabited for centuries by the Sioux.

Here, as in other Sioux communities, were lakes and forests providing vast supplies of fish, game and wild rice. The value of the site was recognized by other tribes, however, and the Sioux were forced to fight hard for their homeland.

The situation changed permanently in 1745 when overwhelming legions of Chippewa attacked the area from Lake Superior. Armed with guns provided by the French, they launched a morning attack just north of Kathio.

Taken by surprise, the Sioux suffered great losses and retreated to the Kathio site where the Chippewa attacked again the following morning in a bloody battle that caused the Sioux to flee once more, this time to an island on Lake Mille Lacs where they made a gallant, but losing, stand.

The Chippewa remain to this day and the site of the original village is marked within the 9,000-acre Mille Lacs Kathio State Park. Nearby, on land where the battles were fought, is the Mille Lacs Indian Museum where Chippewa craftsmen exhibit their skills and valuable historic relics are preserved by the Minnesota Historical Society.

From Mille Lacs Lake southward there is a rapid shift in cultural attitudes as the north woods gives way to very fertile, rolling farmland. Here the orientation is toward the Minneapolis-St. Paul metropolitan complex, whereas northward exists an independent outlook toward the rest of Minnesota that becomes, at times, almost defiant.

The environment must certainly be a major reason for this, requiring a certain self-confidence and ingenuity to survive comfortably in it. Politicians walk tightropes when wooing votes from northern resort areas and the iron ranges—traditional party affiliations are held in less regard than the expected effect of particular candidates.

Linking the Twin Cities with the great north woods area is Interstate Highway 35. As with other modern freeways, it tends to promote a homogeniety of thinking simply through ease of contact. In this case, its connection of Duluth and the Twin Cities has diminished the port city's isolation considerably.

But any exit from the freeway, for those who care to slow down, leads to historic and scenic treasures that abound along the old routes . . . places such as Moose Lake, a charming community of Swiss chalet store fronts; Connors Fur Post near Pine City—a restoration of a voyageur trading center established when Napoleon was conducting triumphant marches across Europe; the Carlos Avery wildlife area near Forest Lake, and the appealing blend of farms and forests that lie between the hills.

Nearby, too, is the magnificent St. Croix River which forms a natural boundary with Wisconsin. Formed by drainage from a glacial melt, its waters are deep and clean and teeming with fish of all kinds. Its unspoiled beauty is likely to continue as it is protected by the federal government under the Wild Rivers Act.

And on the St. Croix, only 25 miles from St. Paul, is the city of Stillwater, the "birthplace of Minnesota."

When Wisconsin became a state in 1848 a triangle of land, previously part of Wisconsin Territory, was not included in the boundaries. This quirk in government planning left the triangle's residents without protection, mail service or roads.

In an unusual public meeting known as the Stillwater Convention of 1848, sixty-one delegates called on Congress and the President to form a Territory of Minnesota. Until the proposal became a reality one year later, the no-man's land formed its own government and was, for all practical purposes, another country.

Like many other towns, Stillwater grew as a lumbering center and was the leading lumbering community in the territory for nearly half a century until competition from wilderness areas transferred superiority to towns further north.

Today, of course, the bulk of all economic activity is found in nearby Minneapolis and in the capitol city of St. Paul, whose combined area harbors a full third of Minnesota's entire population. This in itself provides the most dramatic contrast in a region filled with them.

Within a day's driving time one can attend a performance at the internationally famous Tyrone Guthrie Theatre or stalk a moose in the trackless marshes of Finland State Forest; watch trains of grain-filled barges navigate the locks on the Mississippi or paddle a silent canoe through the maze of rocky cliffs decorated with prehistoric Indian pictographs; walk among the classrooms of one of the country's largest university campuses or visit a one-room mission school on an Indian reservation; observe the country from atop a 57-story office building or tour an iron mine a half-mile below the earth.

It is no mystery that entire books have been written about the northeast section of Minnesota alone, and more could be compiled from subjects yet untouched.

Consider the Witch Tree for instance. Twisted and ravaged by centuries of exposure to the north shore elements, it grows out of a formation of solid rock near Grand Portage. Thought to be inhabited by spirits, it was venerated by the Indians who laid gifts of tobacco and vermilion around its gnarled roots. Estimates of its age vary, but 600 years seems to be a minimum.

One can marvel, too, at what prompted the original inhabitants of this land to bury their dead in huge, earthen mounds such as those found near International Falls. The largest one is 45 feet high and has a circumference of 325 feet. More than 12,000 ancient mounds are scattered throughout the state—probably a fraction of the original numbers which have been eroded beyond recognition.

Books can also be devoted to the transformations wrought by the endless processions of seasons—changes probably more elaborate in the northeast than anywhere else and which give Minnesota the subtitle as the "Theatre of Seasons." Sigurd Olson, the famed chronicler of life and nature in northern Minnesota, has used them as the background for volume after volume.

Winters in Minnesota have traditionally been the subject for much jest and exaggeration, much of it fostered by Minnesotans themselves who enhance the image of their own hardiness by arguing whose yard is most deeply buried in snow, or whose thermometer registered the lowest reading.

To be sure, it does get cold in winter. But the old saying about "it ain't the heat, it's the humidity" applies as well to the sub-zero February temperatures. Even at minus thirty degrees, a winter's day in Ely is decidedly more comfortable than one of plus ten degrees in Minneapolis. The difference is in the dry, windless air of the north which urges nearly as much outdoor activity as during the summer.

More people are discovering the joys of strapping on snowshoes or cross-country skis, either of which enable one to discover the eerie beauty of a snowbound wilderness, enveloped in a silent repose broken only occasionally by the ghostly flight of a snowy owl or a startled dash by a hare.

Gone are the throngs of fishermen and resort guests, and traffic is reduced to local forays for provisions or to visit a neighbor— Duluth the great seaport relaxes as the last ships hurry toward the Atlantic before the St. Lawrence Seaway freezes over.

But if one should tire of the season, there is always another just around the corner. With surprising suddenness, spring begins to advance to the tune of newly-melted waters gushing over a fall; greening forests fill with splashes of rainbow colors as the annual wave of warblers returns; wild flowers sprinkle the roadsides and meadows almost overnight, and a gentle rebirth of nature begins to refresh the land and the human spirit.

It must have been during a particularly beautiful and prolonged spring when Israel Garrard saw Minnesota for the first time and decided it was as close to his idea of Eden as he would ever experience.

Yet he came nowhere near the northeast section just described. His particular Minnesota encompasses yet another in the incredible variety the state exhibits. Garrard chose the southeast in which to live, an area still described by some as "the best kept secret" about Minnesota. Why he came may be attributed to some astute, early efforts to attract settlers to the region. Come they did, anchoring their roots, achieving territorial status then turning to thoughts of statehood. To meet minimum population requirements, the legislature as well as enterprising individuals launched publicity campaigns during the 1850's that would be the envy of today's tourism promoters.

Beginning in 1855, for example, immigrants were greeted in New York harbor by an emigration commissioner—hired by the Minnesota territorial legislature—who spoke eloquently of the opportunities awaiting them in that midwest frontier.

Minnesota newspaper editors devoted much space to publicizing their areas and encouraged their eastern counterparts to take Minnesota vacations. Such visits invariably resulted in enthusiastic reports to the home readers about Minnesota's beauty and productivity, and did much to stimulate migration westward.

Land speculators rushed in to purchase surveyed public lands (at a mere $1.25 per acre), plat towns and sell lots at enormous profts. They advertised their merchandise by hiring writers to send articles to major publications, preparing brochures and retaining lecturers to stump the country with slick presentations of Minnesota's promise.

It was probably that sort of promotion which prompted Israel Garrard, a Kentuckian whose family had derived considerable wealth from its land holdings in Ohio, to take a hunting holiday up the Mississippi and into Minnesota.

He found that the product was everything the advertisements extrolled; so much so, in fact, that Garrard stayed to establish the town of Frontenac on the scenic shores of the Mississippi as it widens to form Lake Pepin. The lake is a natural reservoir on the river, formed by the collapse of its banks during the last glacial retreat, and is not a true lake but one and the same with the Mississippi.

Little changed after more than a century, Frontenac is representative of the way in which the lovely lands of the southeast charmed settlers of the Hiawatha Valley. This is the title of the area through which the great Mississippi flows between Minnesota and Wisconsin.

After winding like a huge question mark through the state, the river attains its full majesty by the time it flows into Iowa. Sometimes reaching a width of a mile or more, it carves a broad, fertile valley walled by limestone bluffs towering up to 500 feet. Many have compared it with Germany's Rhine valley, and the resemblance must account at least partially for the heavy population of German peoples in this corner of Minnesota.

The small towns and villages which pepper the countryside would ordinarily have ceased to exist were they located anywhere else. But agriculture remains king and they thrive by providing services to small, family farm operations. Unsuited for large-scale cash cropping, the hilly land supports a healthy dairy industry as well as an abundance of timber.

A continual harvest of logs from the great hardwood forests is just one benefit trees provide. Between Wabasha and LaCrescent, the hillsides bristle with apple orchards and the springtime air of the Hiawatha Valley becomes scented with billions of fragrant blossoms.

Those who love the outdoors and revel in the primitive purity of Minnesota's northern wilds tend to overlook the more domesticated wilderness of the southeast. To be sure, there are few lakes here; no stands of virgin pine haunted by wolves and moose; no muskies or sturgeon lurking in glacial waters; no bears to irk the camper.

Rather, one experiences something akin to a living Walt Disney landscape. Clear, chuckling streams—many of them filled with trout—thread the pastures and fields, running through shady hollows and carving miniature waterfalls from their soft, limestone beds. Surrounding forests reveal stately elms, venerable oaks and sugar maples, with frequent stands of magnificent black walnut in the low areas. Birch, aspen, butternut and hickory add the trim which, in autumn, provides a hardwood color display to rival a Winslow Homer watercolor.

Berries are abundant and rare is the rural household devoid of such homemade delicacies as wild raspberry jelly, wild grape jam (or wine), and blackberry pie—not to mention the springtime treat of natural maple syrup.

Wildlife, in spite of the proximity of humans, is found in great numbers and variety. White-tailed deer are as common as the rabbits and squirrels, while grouse and pheasants grow fat on elderberries and last year's corn. Raccoons whickering in the night attract the inevitable hunter with his yelping hounds, and a myriad of ponds, built by farmers for their huge dairy herds, become resting places for waterfowl migrating down the Mississippi flyway.

The mild climate of the southeast is favorable to other creatures, too, some of them not ordinarily considered part of the normal state fauna. One of these is the curious opossum; another is the rattlesnake. While plentiful enough to attract bounty hunters, the rattlers remain secluded and timid—most dangerous in tall tales fondly promulgated by local residents.

On the human side of the picture, one sees a world fairly simmering with rural charm: wood smoke curling warmly from winter chimneys; windmills spinning with a liquid clunk; cattle, sheep and goats idly grazing the carpeted green slopes; a dusty pickup truck loading sacks of grain at an old feed mill; morning gossip exchanged at a local creamery.

Yet, for all its seeming combination of New England, the Black Forest and Appalachia, there is a more contemporary mood available too. Modern cities and towns are always within reach and back-to-the-landers discover they can retain their cake (a place in the tranquil countryside) and consume it, too (fine medical care, excellent schools, cultural events).

As U.S. highway 61—the very same which runs along the scenic north shore of Superior—winds southeast from St. Paul, it links a series of historic towns hugging the riverbanks of the Hiawatha Valley. Hastings, with its remarkable historic buildings, retains the atmosphere of the steamboat era from which it sprang.

Red Wing, named for an Indian chief of the area, achieved fame for its pottery works, the products of which are now sought as collector's items. Today it is an industrious and scenic city with much to offer the vacationer.

Lake City, best known for its giant fishing pier, sits like a sparkling jewel on Lake Pepin's shores. Welcome signs proudly state that it is the birthplace of water skiing—thanks to Ralph Samuelson who invented the sport there in 1922.

Winona, born as a lumber town and trading center for the valley, now thrives as a manufacturing center and grain market. On the heights overlooking the town is one of the state's natural oddities—sugarloaf bluff. While its geological formation is uncertain, most feel that sugarloaf bluff was simply a chunk of real estate too high to be ground down by retreating glaciers or by the high waters that ensued from their melt. The thick limestone pillar is visible for miles and has become the emblem for the city.

LaCrescent, across the river from LaCrosse, Wisconsin, stakes its livelihood on the lush orchards which give it the name of "Minnesota's Apple Capitol," and local spring and fall festivals celebrate the importance of that sweet fruit.

In spite of the character displayed by the river towns—or, for that matter, by the rest of the region—tourism has not been an important factor in their economies. Although there are travel facilities and fishing resorts along the river, the bulk of business is generated by the traffic passing through on its way to the Twin Cities or westward on I-90 toward South Dakota.

Except for the handful of scenery seekers and trout anglers that prefer to keep the southeast their secret, even Minnesotans are more oriented toward the lakes and woods of the north. Some feel it is ignored even by the metropolitan media because of its relative scarcity of big industry, social problems and political controversy.

If there is any truth in that, it certainly doesn't apply to Rochester. Situated 40 miles west of Winona, the city is in the transition belt between the hill country just described and the level, slightly rolling lands that ultimately become the prairies of southwest Minnesota.

When Doctor William Mayo began medical practice in Rochester in 1865, it was the central grain depot for southern Minnesota and a primary market for the wheat which was the agricultural mainstay at that time. But as the doctor and his sons, William James (1861-1939) and Charles Horace (1865-1939), began to revolutionize medical procedures, the city found itself expanding to service the throngs who came for treatment. And while Rochester is today a highly industrialized city, the focus of its economy still rests with the celebrated Mayo Clinic and the patients which stream through it from all parts of the globe.

Westward from here, other communities still rely on farming for much of their support. As the land changes from hilly, clay soils to level, loamy ones, corn, soybeans and staple grains are grown as cash crops. There is diversification, too, with beef, pork and poultry supplying the meat packing industries of Austin, Albert Lea and other towns. Coupled with a good dose of manufacturing, and the proximity of road and rail transportation, this makes southeastern Minnesota communities among the most prosperous.

Many of these—Faribault, Waseca, Owatonna, Shakopee and Jordan, to name a few—come very close to the typical ideal of an American small town. All reflect an enviable stability in their slow but steady growth, their low crime rates, their cleanliness and their genuine hospitality. These are the places where hometown baseball teams still generate good Sunday crowds; where the chamber of commerce meets over coffee at the corner cafe; where the annual county fair is the year's big event.

Because of the numerous rivers and streams in southeast Minnesota, few self-respecting towns can get along without one flowing through or at least nearby. One of the most beautiful waterways is the Root River, which runs from a point south of Rochester to empty into the Mississippi by the Winnebago Indian Reservation.

Looking like a miniature Mississippi itself, the Root snakes through ramparts of limestone and pastoral vistas that make it one of the state's most colorful canoe routes. Following its convolutions is U.S. highway 16 which guides the traveller through picture-book towns like Houston, Rushford, Chatfield, Preston and Lanesboro.

No less than a dozen state parks pepper this relatively small section of Minnesota, each preserving a sample of it for generations to come, and nearly a third of its area is managed as state forest land. The department of Natural Resources maintains the state's largest trout hatchery here to stock streams not ordinarily able to sustain permanent fish populations; at the same time, the agency works on "rebuilding" those streams so they can be self-sufficient. Thus, with a growing appreciation of the natural resources here, there has evolved considerable machinery for managing them.

There is also a healthy interest among southern Minnesotans in preserving their historic treasures, which are particularly plentiful. While lacking the sweeping color of Viking and voyageur legacies, it is a showcase for much that is important regarding its pioneer origins.

In Pickwick, for example, a century-old water mill still grinds feed for local farmers while village youngsters splash in the mill pond (incidentally, the town was named for the Pickwick Papers, a popular Dickens' work at the time English settlers organized the community).

In Forestville State Park near Preston, one can walk through the Meighan general store which closed its doors in 1910 after 57 years of trading. Recently opened to the public, it is a true museum containing all the original shelf stock.

Bullet holes in the walls of what was once the Northfield Bank are fondly maintained—relics of the historic gun battle that demolished the Jesse James gang in 1876. The incident is recreated each year to remind visitors that Minnesota was once as much a part of the old west as Kansas and Missouri.

Near Homer, just a few miles downriver from Winona, is the 125-year old home of Willard Bunnell, Indian trader, land speculator and townsite planner. Considered the finest "old house" tour in the state, it is the pride of Winona County's historical society.

Near Shakopee, just southwest of Minneapolis, an entire pioneer community has been reconstructed—complete with inhabitants who live and work according to the precepts of another age.

In many ways, southeast Minnesota is comparable to northeast. Both have scenic drives (indeed, the same highway—U.S. 61—follows both the north shore and the Hiawatha Valley); both have unique underground attractions—the Tower-Soudan mine up north and the spectacular caves near Harmony; both are endowed with great forest lands, although one has softwoods and the other hardwoods; and each has a large city—Duluth and Rochester—radiating economic influence second only to the Twin Cities.

The differences, of course, outnumber those broad similarities, and one of them is the general political attitudes which have remained basically unchanged since territorial days.

Minnesota as a whole is unpredictable where political elections are concerned. Its list of governors are well balanced between Democrats and Republicans. But while an independent spirit guides things in general, there are regional preferences that are at least semi-permanent. Never were these so evident as when Minnesota was about to become a state.

In drawing up state boundaries, it was understood that the territory was too large and would have to be nearly halved. Since the north favored the Democrats and the south Republicans, several proposals to slice off either the top or bottom of the territory—while extending the lands all the way to the Missouri River in what is now the Dakotas—were introduced.

That Minnesota does not look like Montana today is a tribute to the spirit of compromise that finally prevailed, although not without some humorous incidents of party chauvinism. The most graphic is the fact that Minnesota has two constitutions.

Unwilling to sign any paper to which opposite party members had affixed signatures, the Democrats and Republicans drew separate, original drafts of the state constitution—identical but for the preambles—and both are preserved as the foundation for Minnesota law.

The conservative nature of southern Minnesotans makes them unwilling to discard proven methods until something better has demonstrated its worth. That may explain in part why this corner of the state exists on two levels. On one hand, it is in the mainstream of modern technology and economics; on the other, it retains the genteel rural charm peculiar to the early part of the century.

From this corner of the state came the last westward push of Minnesota pioneers. And in the excitement of settling the rich, lands of the southwest, the tranquil region of hills, forests and streams was left to mature quietly like a half-forgotten cask of old wine.

Words do little to capture the enchantment of such places as Hammond, where one store is a grocery, barber shop, gas station, restaurant and post office combined. . . .

Of Wasioja, the waning hamlet which was once bigger than Rochester, where the only Civil War recruiting station in the state is still preserved. . . .

Of Old Frontenac, where people still come for Sunday services to a church built in 1868 . . . of Pine Island with its cheese factory; Zumbrota with its covered bridge; of the many tiny settlements with such melodious names as Tawny, Pilot Mound, Hope and Money Creek.

Minnesota's personality is ever fluid, often taking surprising turns. Perhaps the last major incident to precipitate yet another transformation in its character was the Treaty of Traverse Des Sioux on the Minnesota River which emanates from the "bump" on her western border. This river flowing in a southeasterly direction, abruptly changes course in Mankato to flow northeast until it joins the Mississippi at St. Paul.

This important junction was selected as the site for Fort Snelling, the first outpost of the U. S. Military in Minnesota. Completed in 1823 after more than three years of construction, the fort was established to protect the fur trade and keep peace in the northlands (today Fort Snelling looks exactly as it did then, thanks to a monumental, decade-long project of restoration by the Minnesota Historical Society). It fulfilled its mission admirably, living up to its motto: "never a shot fired in anger."

For decades this outpost was the symbol of civilization in Minnesota's wilderness. It was the gathering place not only for politicians and missionaries, but for fur traders, explorers, artists, writers and scientists as well. The Indians, too, held it in high regard and viewed it as a place of refuge and a source of help.

It was only natural that some of these visitors would become permanent settlers, and by 1840 an entirely new community had sprung from the shadows of the fort across the river. Originally called "Pig's Eye" (for an unsavory bootlegger who was the first settler), it was home for many French-speaking Catholics. To serve them, a young priest named Lucien Galtier was called from his native France to the Minnesota wilds.

The "pioneer priest", as historians refer to him, built a crude log church for his new parishioners and dedicated it to St. Paul, the "apostle of nations." In 1863 it was renamed St. Peter's Church and replaced with a stone structure—but by that time it had provided the name for Minnesota's capitol city of St. Paul.

St. Paul's sister city of Minneapolis is not without its own historic clerical figures. Chief among these is Father Louis Hennepin, a Belgian frair who, in 1680, discovered a majestic waterfall which he named for St. Anthony of Padua, his patron saint. Hennepin was among the earliest explorers of the upper Mississippi River, and his adventures included capture by the Sioux, who held him prisoner for several months.

Streets, buildings and a county bear Hennepin's name today, but what would have been the most appropriate monument has disappeared. St. Anthony Falls has been reduced to a mere concrete spillway on the Mississippi as it flows through Minneapolis.

The goodwill that developed between Minnesota's Sioux tribes and the white men can be attributed largely to the work of Major Lawrence Taliaferro (pronounced Tol'-iver), Indian Agent at the fort for twenty years. A staunch advocate of Indians' rights, he protected them from exploitation by traders, settled disputes between tribes, helped them establish schools and agriculture, and respected their customs and beliefs. He inspired in them a confidence in white men that lasted for decades.

During the summer of 1851 territorial and federal officials met with the various Sioux tribes at Traverse Des Sioux to negotiate a treaty for the lands of southwest Minnesota, northwest Iowa and South Dakota. After a month of talk and festivity, the Sioux relinquished 24 million acres of their hereditary domain for just over $1.6 million.

Little of that money ever reached Indian hands, however, and the betrayal of trust led to the eventual eruption of all-out war in the Minnesota River valley.

Prior to that tragedy, however, the southwest region flowered with a steady influx of hardy pioneering souls who cultivated the fertile prairie soil and filled the open spaces with villages and towns. Czechs, Dutch and Germans were the area's chief populators and communi-

ties like Luverne, Windom and Montgomery still reflect the spirit of those determined nationalities.

With the exception of rolling, lake-studded landscapes on the north side of the Minnesota River, there is little resemblance here to other regions of the state. Forest lands are few, consisting mostly of planted farm woodlots or wooded river valleys. The comparatively few lakes are small and shallow, and wildlife is limited to the smaller species such as rabbits and pheasant.

It is basically a tranquil prairie region, a typical setting for a Willa Cather novel. Its economy—other than in the more industrialized cities along Interstate 90 as it skirts the Iowa border—is heavily agricultural. Apart from crops of corn, wheat and soybeans, large tracts are devoted to sweet corn, peas, beans and other truck crops. Dairying is important but beef and poultry operations share the billing.

Until recent years, the tourism/travel trade was of little significance here, although lakeside resorts around such areas as Glencoe, Willmar and Montevideo have traditionally catered to a respectable summer business. The western area attracts autumn visitors who come to hunt the plentiful pheasant and waterfowl of the upper Minnesota valley.

The prime attraction of the area, however, is not in such typical outdoor recreation opportunities; it is, instead, the deep-rooted Indian traditions and lore that color its history.

Perhaps the single, best-known site is the Pipestone National Monument near Pipestone, just nine miles from the South Dakota border. It is here that a unique, auburn-colored rock called catlinite—or, more commonly, pipestone—has been quarried by various Indian nations for more than seven centuries.

Pipestone was highly revered among Indians throughout the country and was used primarily for the ceremonial pipes used by the Plains tribes and others. These famous "peace pipes" were exactly that. They were used to end quarrels between tribes and individuals, to strengthen alliances or to seal agreements. If a pipe was offered and accepted in battle, both sides retired their weapons and peace was restored.

Such a peace was seldom violated, since the Great Spirit would surely punish the troublemaker. It was He, according to Indian beliefs, who had presented the red pipestone to warring Indian nations and charged them to smoke peace pipes in order to restore good will.

In 1937 an act of Congress established the quarries as a national monument, preserving the rights of all tribes to use them. Only American Indians are allowed to mine pipestone under special permits issued by the National Park Service.

Remnants of more ancient Indian cultures are scattered throughout southwest Minnesota—remnants so old that even today's Indians cannot fathom their meanings. One of these occurs on a low ridge just 20 miles east of Pipestone.

Here, laid out with stones in the middle of a field, is the figure of a huge buffalo and, not far away, the outline of a man. Both are discernible only from the air and are unexplainable in terms of known Indian beliefs and legends.

And about 40 miles east of Pipestone, near the little town of Jeffers, are the mysterious petroglyphs (from Greek words meaning "rock carving"). Here one finds countless pictures scratched on rocks, depicting deer, turtles, birds, humans and parts of human figures. Others are mere symbols, lines and abstract forms undecipherable today. Even their age is unclear, with estimates ranging from hundreds to thousands of years.

Archaeologists believe the carvings were done over a long period of time by many different tribes. The pictures could have been their method of illustrating legends, communicating with their Gods, or perhaps just idle doodling. No one knows.

The amiable relationship between white men and Indians in Minnesota came very close to being unmarred, even after Indians had relinquished their vast southwest lands in 1851. The work of Lawrence Taliaferro had fostered mutual respect, an attitude accepted by most settlers. Some may argue that peace would have continued had Minnesotans been in sole charge of their Indian affairs.

Peaceful coexistence, however, was shattered during the summer of 1862 after repeated failures of the U.S. Government to provide either goods or payments in accordance with the treaty. Left without their traditional hunting lands (the Sioux were allowed a ten-mile wide strip along the Minnesota River), the Indians' frustration suddenly found release in attacks on the Indian agencies near Granite Falls and Morton.

Without detailing events—these are appropriately covered in other works—it will suffice to say that the incidents opened a "second front" for a U.S. Army already preoccupied with the Civil War.

The Sioux were driven westward from Minnesota in only a few months, but not before leaving permanent scars on Minnesota's communities and providing chapters in historical volumes that twinge the conscience.

Today a traveler can relive the Sioux conflict by simply following the Minnesota River between Montevideo and Mankato. Mingled with the serene beauty of the wooded valleys, and the quiet villages perched along the river banks, are grim but fascinating reconstructions of that turbulent year.

The Upper Sioux Agency, for example, has been preserved as part of a state park. Once the home of a treacherous agent who refused Indians food from the bulging supply house, it is a pleasant stop for canoeists or campers. The Lower Sioux Agency, also sacked and burned, is today an interpretive center for Sioux history.

Other battle sites are maintained, too, such as that at Birch Coulee near Morton. An Indian-cavalry skirmish occurred here which provided all the elements of the standard western movie portrayals—

outnumbered soldiers firing from behind their dead mounts, repeated dawn attacks, and the last-minute rescue by reinforcements. The site is marked in detail for those who want to generate the feel of those extremely tense moments.

Fort Ridgely, the object of an unsuccessful, three-day attack, has also been reconstructed as part of a state park. Here, battles are described in detail by markers as one walks around the historic buildings.

In the city of New Ulm, the only major town to come under serious attack, is a monument to its defenders. It is hard to imagine this beautiful community as it must have been then, with street barricades, burning buildings and the smoke and cry of battle. Incidentally Doctor Charles Mayo was in the thick of it, caring for the wounded. He was not to move to Rochester until three years later.

In Mankato, the largest city in the region, the final tragic incident took place as 38 Indians accused of "war crimes" were executed in December, 1862. Although 303 had been convicted, President Lincoln commuted the sentences of the rest. It was the largest legal execution in the history of the country, a record that instills very little pride among anyone today.

Of course the history of this Minnesota frontier was not all gloom and bloodshed. With the exception of that brief period, life consisted of breaking new ground, watching the railroads come through, building towns and developing industry.

One adventuresome spirit who participated in all these was Joseph R. Brown, who came to Minnesota as a drummer boy at Fort Snelling. He was already in Taylors Falls when the first lumbermen arrived to establish a sawmill. He was one of those present at the Stillwater meeting of 1848 to help establish the Minnesota territory. Always in the vanguard of any pioneers, he started moving westward very early. Shortly after the 1851 treaty he founded the town of Henderson, just a few miles above Traverse Des Sioux.

Long before any white settlements existed in the southwest, Brown was there in grand style. By 1860 he and his family had built a three-story, pink granite mansion furnished with such items as two grand pianos, crystal chandeliers and damask drapery—all situated on the Minnesota River 100 miles west of St. Paul!

In August of 1862 Brown was in New York trying to sell his idea for a "steam wagon" (Sinclair Lewis later wrote that he was, as much as anyone, the inventor of the automobile). During his absence, the Indian troubles erupted and his mansion was destroyed. The ruins remain as part of a state wayside below Granite Falls.

With the return of peace, he moved further west to settle in what is now Browns Valley, the westernmost town in Minnesota, where he operated a stagecoach line.

Such are the personalities which fill the pages of southern Minnesota's history and many little-known communities can claim some historic relationship with them.

Garden City has a building erected by Henry Wellcome, a town native who aided Stanley in his famed search for Livingston.

The great race horse, Dan Patch, was raised and trained in Savage, a town subsequently named for his owner, Marion Savage.

Both Madelia and St. James share the spot where the Younger Brothers were captured after helping Jesse James with the aborted Northfield bank caper.

LeSueur calls itself the home of giants, referring to its being the first home of Doctor Charles Mayo and, more recently, the headquarters for the Jolly Green Giant whose company logo has created a legend not unlike that of Paul Bunyan.

Visitors to this area are often surprised that the giant's valley is really more than just a television gimmick. And one glance at the lush, green fields of vegetables in LeSueur is enough to prompt an expectation of a "ho-ho-ho" ringing through the hills.

Because southwest Minnesota has always depended on agriculture for its economic well-being, it has experienced the effects of rural outmigration more vividly than have other state regions. The flight of people to cities, coupled with the growth of large scale, corporate farming, have left some communities floundering.

While the country-to-city trend seems to be reversing now, it is difficult for many once attractive towns to make a comeback. But the pioneering spirit is still alive and several afflicted areas have been rejuvenated in recent years, either through concerted efforts to attract industry or by developing attractions for tourists.

In the latter category, "developing" often means informing the public of what already exists. Browns Valley is a case in point. Of less than 1,000 population, it is frequently bypassed by travellers who prefer a straight north-south route rather than follow the bump in Minnesota's backside. Consequently, many miss a delightful drive on Hwy 27 which provides sweeping vistas of two river valleys as they spread out to become the plains of South Dakota.

There is a geographical curiosity here, too. The Red River, which flows north, begins at this point as does the southward flowing Minnesota. If one tipped the state so that its western border were on top, it would be two rivers running down opposite sides of a hill.

Many attractive rivers flow quietly through the cultivated countryside, among them the Blue Earth River. Named for the colorful clay of its banks, its bluish mud was used by the Indians as war paint.

At the upper end of the Minnesota River is a reservoir named by early French explorers. They called it Lac qui Parle, literally meaning "lake that talks" because of the clamor of waterfowl arising from its waters. Today it is part of Lac qui Parle Wildlife Area.

Fifty miles east lies the resort area of New London and Spicer. Fishing is the big attraction here, especially on Green Lake, called by some the cleanest lake in the world (on a calm day one can count the pebbles resting thirty feet below its surface).

By this time it should be apparent why Minnesota cannot be described with any brevity. The many facets of its character are not revealed by such long-used phrases as "land of woods and waters," or "theatre of seasons," or, as one tongue-in-cheek phrasemaker has said, "Minnie with the iron bottom." It is all these things, of course, but the popular conceptions fall short of the real article.

Long-standing myths also color the picture. One of these is the so-called severity of Minnesota winters, an idea reinforced by a perennial reference to winter temperatures in International Falls. Yet the total annual snowfall averages an unspectacular 42 inches while the average winter temperature is about twenty degrees—Farenheit.

Another notion is that Minnesota's character is primarily rural oriented, with the only substantial industry confined to the Twin City metropolitan area. In reality, two-thirds of the state's 3.8 million people live in urban areas, with industrial growth and expansion occurring at a faster pace in the non-Twin Cities area. Also, fourteen of the nation's 500 largest corporations are headquartered in the state, including some of the best known electronics and computer firms.

And for those who think Minnesota is negotiable only via gravelled roads or snowmobile trails, the truth is that its splendid roads and highways—nearly 130,000 miles of them—rank fifth among the states.

Not generally realized, either, is Minnesota's leadership in education with nearly 100 junior colleges, liberal arts colleges and universities, and area vocational-technical schools. Healthwise, its citizens live longer and require less medical aid than most other U.S. inhabitants according to various insurance company statistics.

Some things cannot be measured so easily, however, and it is by such standards that Minnesotans still judge the quality of their lives. How does one place a value on the sight of a bald eagle soaring above the green Hiawatha Valley forests? Or on the primitive thrill of hearing a howling timber wolf in the wintry northern wilderness?

There is a certain zest for life exhibited by Minnesotans, inspired, perhaps, by having ready access to more than 15,000 lakes, 15,000 miles of rivers and streams, millions of acres of forest, clean air, scenery in limitless abundance, and four seasons to provide constant change and continual refreshing of the spirit.

But even Minnesotans often take these riches for granted. Sometimes a clearer appreciation is expressed by visitors who see the Gopher State for the first time. The state's tourism office in St. Paul not only disseminates information, it receives it as well.

Among thousands of such letters on file is one from a sixth grade boy in California. In two simple sentences, it says more than a volume:

"I think Minnesota is the most beautiful state of all. I would like to come and live there."

Surging water of the Pigeon River drops
105 feet near the Canadian border along extreme
northeast corner of state.

Sheer granite cliffs along shore of
Lake Superior near Beaver Bay. This is largest
body of fresh water in the world.

Petroglyph carved by Indians over 600 years
ago in stone outcroppings near Jeffers.

Lone horse provides sharp contrast to
brilliant blue water of pond near Lake Elmo.

Last remnants of winter
disappear as apple buds begin to mature.

Pigeon River cascades into granite gorge
generating wind-blown mist adhering to protective
netting along the rim.

Exploring the Boundary Waters Canoe Area
near Canadian border in Superior National Forest.

Walter library on campus of the University
of Minnesota in Minneapolis. This land-grant school
was established by the territorial legislature in 1851.

Plum blossom releases the last sign of winter to greet
the glorious days of spring that lie ahead.

Berger Fountain in Loring Park
on the edge of downtown Minneapolis.
Ever changing skylines never
cease to be impressive.

Blocks of ice form palatial house in St. Paul
during Winter Carnival. This annual event was born
at the turn of the century. Pages 40 and 41:
Dense foliage gives clear definition of Caribou Lake
in central Cook County.

Minnehaha Falls immortalized in
Longfellow's "Hiawatha". An area of picturesque
charm in Minnehaha Park, within the city
limits of Minneapolis.

Colorful foliage spells the
arrival of autumn along the St. Croix River.

Chilling winter storm envelops dense
stand of spruce trees in Superior National Forest.

Snow encrusted branch
of white spruce in Cook County.
An area of rugged forests and wide array of wildlife.

Mid-winter along the north shore of Lake Superior.
Nearby is some of the most primitive wilderness
remaining in the world today.

Unusual ice formation on Temperance River will
eventually give way to the entrance of spring.

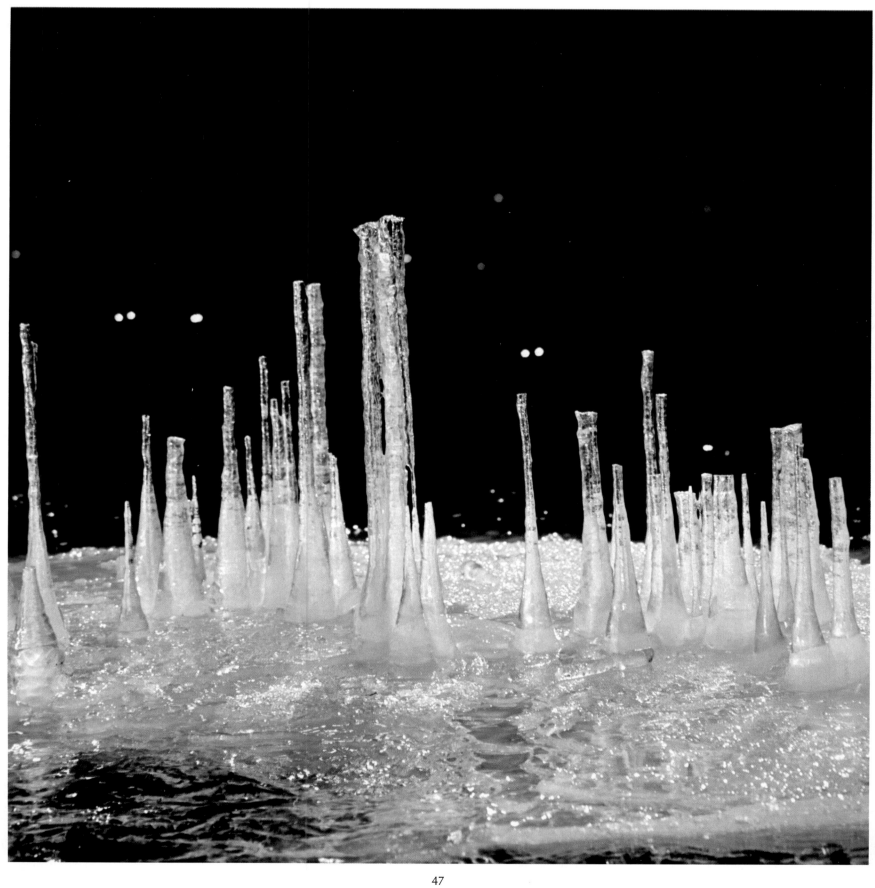

Norway Pines, the state tree, soar
skyward on crest of hill in Itasca State Park.

Temperance River gorge marked with
signs of winter below Last Wilderness Falls.

Sun bathers relaxing on sandy
shore of the Zumbro River at Zumbro Falls.

Jack-in-the-pulpit hails the
arrival of spring in many wooded areas.

Silo lends brilliant contrast to spring
foliage along Highway 16 near Preston.

Bluebells carpet a gentle slope
above the Root River near Houston.

The Capitol in St. Paul clearly
displays its architectural embellishments on
this lovely mid-winter day.

Kayaker passing sheer granite wall anticipating more turbulent water on the St. Croix River. Pages 56 and 57: Wave explodes along north shore of Lake Superior. In background the Sawtooth Mountains.

The Mayo Clinic in Rochester. These modern buildings reflect the refinement and accuracy of the dedicated medical staff serving patients from every land.

Pastoral scene near the
Wisconsin border in early evening.

Sled dogs await their master's
command at training site near Ely.

Lady's Slipper—Minnesota State flower.
A member of the orchid family, it is seldom seen
due to its limited growing areas.

Fort Snelling at the junction of the Minnesota
and Mississippi Rivers. Established in 1820 it was here
that Count Zeppelin, German military observer
with the Union Army, conducted
experiments in balloon flying in 1864.

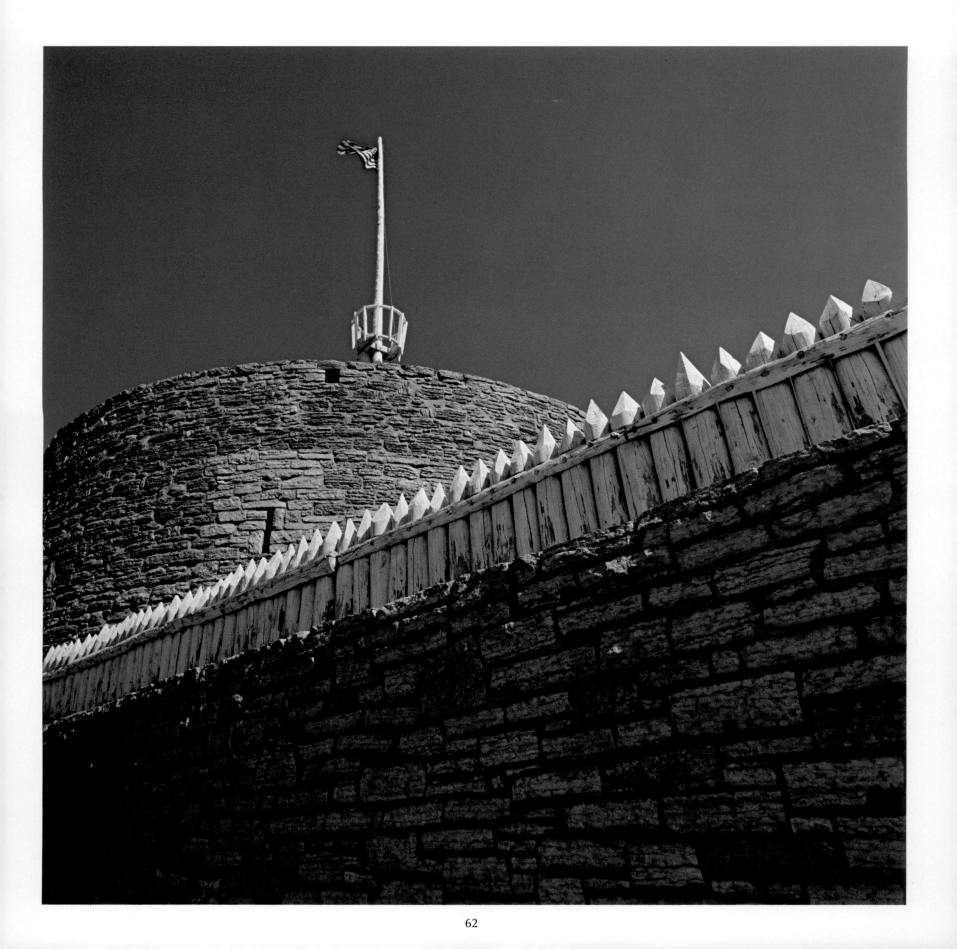

Leaping Rocks, Pipestone National Monument.
Indian braves would vault to this stone formation
proving their manhood to an interested maiden.

Age old log house appears structurally sound
destined to stand for eons.

Spring foliage delivers a maximum of cheerfulness
near Houston.

Light layer of fog blankets the hills and valleys
in Washington County, south of Marine on St. Croix.

Hidden Falls appears as strips of ribbon
in Summit Parkway north of St. Paul.

Sheet ice develops an incredible formation
on the St. Croix River near Sunrise in Chisago County.

St. Croix River flowing gently past the town
of Stillwater. Established in 1843, it is identified
as the oldest community within the state.

Quiet reflections on the glasslike surface
of Lake Lamay, near Mendota, southwest of St. Paul.

Barn and silo identify with the importance of
agriculture on this farm near shore of
Minnesota River.

Seemingly endless ribbons of hay lie on the gently
undulating hills of Olmstead County.

Oat, heads laden with drops of rain, create
and interesting pattern.

Giant icicles create major ice mass along
upper reaches of Lake Superior.

Ice encrusted rocks offer brilliant contrast to
the frigid water of Lake Superior.

North American timber wolf assumes a docile
stance in Superior National Forest. Hounded by man
from time immemorial, significant numbers may
be found only in Alaska and Minnesota.

Sheer rock wall rises abruptly from shore
of Whitewater River.

Water of St. Croix River bathes the shifting sands
along its lower reaches.

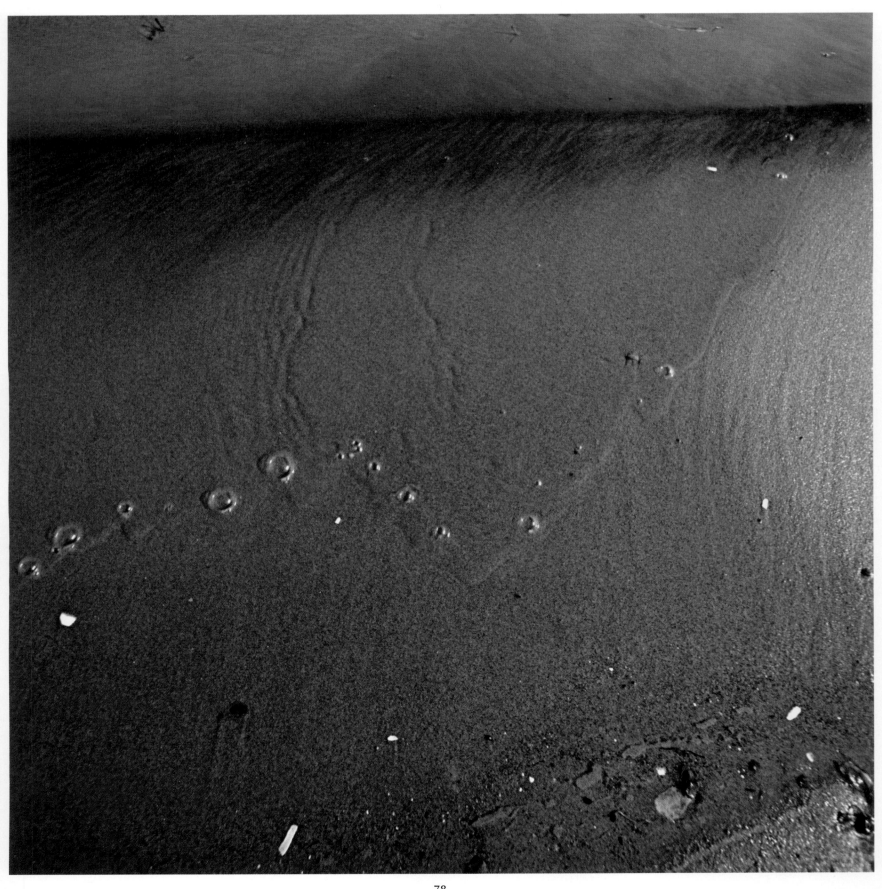

White tail deer acts very docile in its native habitat.
Bear, otter, the elusive fisher, moose and
waterfowl of many descriptions also live here.

Blanket of snow provides satinlike surface
on rolling hill near Afton.

Frost coats scattered pines and poplars
covering erratic terrain near Britton Peak
along the Sawbill Trail in Cook County.

Clusters of berries on limbs of
Mountain Ash, a species of tree belonging to the
rose family. It is a small tree that reaches its
greatest size on the northern shores of
Lakes Huron and Superior.

Willows and water grass abound along shore
of small lake near South St. Paul.

Lone cedar maintains a silent vigil along the
north shore of Lake Superior. Named the "Witch
Tree", its gray and weathered trunk repels the
wild tempests that rip this rocky shore.

Wheat fields and plumes of water from irrigation
system seem so very fresh and exciting in the
Red River Valley.

Intriguing Alexander Calder mobile outside Walker
Art Center near downtown area of Minneapolis.

Grotesque formation along underground passage of
Niagra Cave near Harmony. Pages 88 and 89:
Dairy cattle grazing on productive pasture land
north of Rochester.

Looking northwest over summit of Eagle Mountain
(2,301 feet) the highest peak in Minnesota.

The chill of winter seems to have completely
enveloped the Manitou River near Little Marais.

Morning sun defines the arrival of spring across a
rolling pasture area along an obscure country
road near Caledonia.

Oak trees and sumac draped in their
autumn foliage in the area of Lake Minnetonka.

Ice along shore of Lake Superior near Two Harbors
northeast of Duluth.

Plowed field reveals the rich fertile soil that is so
abundant in the Red River Valley; reaching
depths of 15 feet or more.

Splitrock lighthouse on shore of Lake Superior once
warned ships of dangerous reefs near Beaver Bay.

Deer appears alert at base of sharp ridge in
Blue Mounds State Park near Luverne. An area dotted
by many irregular glacial hills and rocky ridges.

Broad expanse of Lake Itasca around whose
perimeter was developed a state park.

Pine trees along Highway I, near Ely, one of several
entrances to the Boundary Waters Canoe Area.

Lady Bird Beetles appear contented near a bed
of wild violets in early spring.

Stone designs on summit of Buffalo Ridge
remain a mystery.

Bison that once thundered across our
prairies in huge numbers are a part of our American
history. Small herds in the upper mid-west
are now making a comeback under
government supervision.

Afterglow of the setting sun creates a
spectacular view in northern area of state.
Pages 104 and 105: Fall colors along St. Croix River
at Stillwater will soon exit, permitting winter
to play its role.

Delicate arms of pasture weed
coated with frost create lacelike pattern.
In background dense grove of birch.

Broad sweep of Superior National Forest seen from
Britton Park along the Sawbill Trail.

Old school house seems determined to survive
long after retirement, near Hector.

Remains of flour mill near Hastings. Erected in 1856,
by Alexander Ramsey, it was destroyed by fire
on Christmas Day 1894.

Delightful old barn appears to be losing the
urge to survive. Erected at the turn of the century
it stands alone on farm in Renville County.

Liverwort growing in limestone crags.
Southeastern Minnesota's Memorial Hardwood
Forest provides the proper environment for
an array of woodland images.

Fallen trees, limbs, moss and foliage present
a contemporary masterpiece.

Swimmers enjoy the invigorating aspects of
Lake Winnibigoshish, along the southeast shore.

Children wading in the out flow of
Lake Itasca, that launches the mighty Mississippi
River on its lengthy descent. Approximately
forty-one percent of the United States sends
its waters by this vast system to the Gulf of Mexico.

Stone arch bridge erected by James J. Hill in
1382-83. It is the oldest mainline railroad span of its
type to cross the Mississippi River. In the distance
skyline of downtown Minneapolis.

Chain of lakes in Superior National Forest
along the Minnesota, Canadian border near Ontario.

Canadian Geese pause for pleasant repast during winter migration at Roseau River Wildlife Refuge near Pine Creek. Birds, waterfowl, deer and moose find shelter here on more than 50,000 acres of land.

This well preserved Hill Mansion in St. Paul
is perhaps one of Minnesota's most dominant homes.
Erected in 1889, the interior contains priceless
furnishings and imported wood carvings.

Clear winter morning along the Stony river
delivers an aura of brilliance. Pages 120 and 121:
Apple blossoms announce the arrival
of spring in a Hiawatha Valley orchard near
La Crescent.

Chimney Rock continues to defy the forces of nature,
south of Hastings in Dakota County.

St. Croix River, the last metropolitan riverway
in the United States whose natural qualities
are still basically unspoiled.

Aerial view captures gentle stream weaving
its way through a farming area.

Apple blossom, heralds the arrival of spring in
orchard on outskirts of La Crescent.

Stream tumbles through a forest corridor along
canoe portage into East-Bearskin Lake.

Morning sun renders an unusual mood
in early spring.